READ AND SHARE™

Bible

For:

_____

From:

_____

Date:

_____

Give thanks to the Lord and pray to him.
Tell the nations what he has done.
Sing to him. Sing praises to him.
Tell all the wonderful things he has done.
Be glad that you are his.
Let those who ask the Lord for help be happy.
Depend on the Lord and his strength.
Always go to him for help.
Remember the wonderful things he has done.
Remember his miracles and his decisions. . . .
He will keep his promises always.

PSALM 105:1–5, 8

READ AND SHARE™
Bible

More Than 200 Best-Loved Bible Stories

Stories Retold by
Gwen Ellis

Illustrated by Steve Smallman

Tommy NELSON®

A Division of Thomas Nelson Publishers
Since 1798

www.thomasnelson.com

READ AND SHARE™ BIBLE

Published in Nashville, Tennessee, by Tommy Nelson®, a division of Thomas Nelson, Inc., in association with Lion Hudson plc.

Stories based on *The Holy Bible, International Children's Bible®*, copyright © 1986, 1988, 1999, 2005 by Tommy Nelson®, a division of Thomas Nelson, Inc.

Stories retold by Gwen Ellis
Illustrated by Steve Smallman

Tommy Nelson® books may be purchased in bulk for educational, business, fundraising, or sales promotional use. For information, please email SpecialMarkets@ThomasNelson.com.

Library of Congress Cataloging-in-Publication Data

Ellis, Gwen.
  Read and share Bible : more than 200 best-loved Bible stories / by Gwen Ellis.
      p. cm.
  ISBN-13: 978-1-4003-0853-8 (hardback)
  ISBN-10: 1-4003-0853-4 (hardback)
  1. Bible stories, English. I. Title.
BS551.3.E55 2007
220.9'505—dc22
                            2006029401

Worldwide co-edition produced by
Lion Hudson plc,
Mayfield House, 256 Banbury Road,
Oxford OX2 7DH, England
Telephone: +44 (0) 1865 302750
Fax: +44 (0) 1865 302757
Email: coed@lionhudson.com
www.lionhudson.com

Printed in USA
07 08 09 10 QWV 5 4 3 2

For Paige

Dear Parents

What you are holding in your hands is not just a book; it's a unique way to share God's Word with the children in your life, a way to help them come to know God's love, goodness, and faithfulness to us . . . and to share that good news with others.

In today's fast-paced world, it's not easy to carve out special times together with family. But it's my hope that the 208 bite-size stories in this book will enable you to make the most out of those important times together.

As I selected the stories for *Read and Share™ Bible*, I decided to include, not only well-known Bible stories, but also some that rarely appear in Bible storybooks. They, too, are significant in understanding God's love. The stories are also in chronological order to show children how the whole Bible fits together. Based on *The Holy Bible, International Children's Bible*®, each story has a Scripture reference to make it easy for you to read more about the story from the Bible. (Check out the tips on the following page for more helpful ways to use this book.)

God bless you and the children in your life as together you get to know Him better through the pages of this book.

Blessings,
Gwen Ellis

Tips on How to Use This Book

- Read these stories aloud to your children. Dramatize the story as you read. Make the lions *roar* and the thunder *boom*. The kids will love it, listen, respond, and remember. Older children will benefit from reading the story independently in addition to hearing it read aloud.

- When the story is over, discuss the questions, thoughts, and extra information in the boxes at the end of the stories. These sharing and discussion prompts make this Bible storybook unique, and they help the child to focus on the real meanings of the stories. Don't miss out on this important feature.

- Use the book as a tool to help refresh your memory of favorite stories. You may even hear one you haven't heard before. Either way, embrace it as a learning experience for both you and your child.

- Use *Read and Share*™ *Bible* stories as part of a family Bible study, in Sunday school classes, for bedtime, or for any other special reading time with children.

Contents

xiii

Old Testament

The First Day

Genesis 1:1–5

In the beginning God made heaven and earth. At first it was empty and dark. But God gathered up the light and called it *day*.

Then He gathered up the darkness and called it *night*. God was watching over everything.

What do you think God did next?

The Second Day

Genesis 1:6–8

On day two God divided the air from the water. He put some water above the air and some below it. He named the air *sky*.

The next day God made something many children like, especially in the summer. Can you guess what it is?

The Third Day

Genesis 1:9–13

On day three God was busy. He made puddles and oceans and lakes and waterfalls and rivers. He made the dry ground too.

Next He made plants. He made so many different kinds of trees, flowers, and bushes, that no one could count them all. God said His work was good.

Wow! God made so much on that day.
But can you guess what was missing?

The Fourth Day

Genesis 1:14–19

On day four God put the sun in the sky to warm the earth. He saw that the night was very dark, so God put the moon and the stars in the sky.

8

Then God made spring, summer, fall, and winter. All that He made was good.

Next God made flippy, flappy fun things.
Let's see what they were.

The Fifth Day

Genesis 1:20–23

On day five God made starfishes, octopuses, whales, and turtles. He made fast little fish for rivers and slippery big fish for the ocean.

He made big birds like eagles to soar in the sky and zippy little birds like hummingbirds. He made birds in all shapes, sizes, and colors.

**Which bird do you think is the prettiest?
Which is the strongest?**

The Sixth Day

Genesis 1:24–31

On day six God made the animals—
puppies, cows, horses, kitties, bears,
lizards, mice, worms, and lots more.
Everything was good.

But something was still missing. There were no people. So God made some. And when He made them, He made them like Himself. He made them so they could be friends with Him.

Where do you think the first people lived?

Adam and Eve

Genesis 2:1–5, 15–22; 3:20

God named the first man Adam. God put
Adam in a beautiful garden. He gave him
all the animals. He gave him all the fish
and the birds too.

Then God gave Adam one more thing.
God made a woman to be Adam's wife.
Adam named his wife Eve. On day seven
God rested from all His work.

**Uh-oh. Something bad was about to happen
on the earth.**

The Sneaky Snake

Genesis 2:16–17; 3:1–6

God gave Adam and Eve one rule. "Eat anything you like except the fruit from the tree in the middle of the garden."

16

A sneaky old snake came to Eve. "Eat it, then you'll know everything, just like God." So Eve ate the fruit and gave some to Adam. And he ate it too.

When we disobey God, it's called *sin*. There are always consequences when we disobey.

Out of the Garden

Genesis 3:8–24

One evening God came to visit Adam and Eve. But they were hiding. When God found them, He asked, "What have you done?" Adam told God everything. God was sad.

Because they had disobeyed God, Adam and Eve had to leave the beautiful garden. When they were outside of the garden, Adam and Eve had to work very hard to grow food.

**It makes God very sad when we disobey.
It makes our parents sad too.**

Noah

Genesis 6

Many years later there were lots of people on the earth, but most of them were bad. One man—Noah—was good. He obeyed God. "I want you to build a boat," God told Noah.

Noah started right away. People laughed
at Noah because they lived in a desert
and there was no water for his boat.
Noah just went on building
the boat.

21

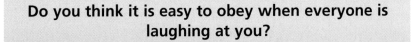

The Big Boat

Genesis 7:1–15

When the boat was finished, God told Noah and his family to go into the boat. In went his sons Shem, Ham, and Japheth. In went their wives and Mrs. Noah.

"Now bring two of every animal," God told Noah. Noah did exactly what God told him to do. And God watched over him.

Something very wet was about to happen outside.

Inside the Boat

Genesis 7:16–24

When the last animal climbed into the boat, God shut the door. *Plip! Plop! Plip!* It began to rain. It rained so much, the water was over the meadows. It rained so much, it covered the towns. It rained so much, it even covered the mountains.

But inside the boat, everyone was safe.

How many days do you think it rained?

The Dove

Genesis 7:12; 8:1–19

After 40 days and 40 nights, the rain stopped, but it still wasn't time to get off the boat. Water was everywhere. One day Noah let a little dove fly out to see what was happening on the earth.

It brought a green leaf back. Hooray! The plants were growing again! It was almost time to come out!

What do you think everyone did when Noah opened the door of the boat?

The Rainbow

Genesis 8:18–22; 9:1–17

When everyone was out of the boat, Noah built an altar. He thanked God for keeping them safe. Then something wonderful happened!

God put a beautiful rainbow in the sky and made Noah a promise. "It will never flood over the whole earth like that again," God said. When God makes a promise, He keeps it.

29

All God's promises are in the Bible. Isn't it wonderful to think of all He has promised us?

Babel

Genesis 11:1–9

Many years later there were lots of people on the earth. They all spoke the same language. Some people who lived in the city of Babel became too proud. "Let's build a tower that reaches to the sky. We'll be famous."

God caused them to speak different languages so they couldn't talk to one another. Because they couldn't understand one another, they stopped building the tower.

Do you have any friends who speak a foreign language? Are you patient with them?

Abram

Genesis 12:1–3; 15:5; 22:17

God picked Abram to be the father of a very important family. One day in the future, Jesus would come from this family.

God told Abram, "I will make you famous. Your children and grandchildren will be as many as the stars. They will be as many as the grains of sand on the beach. You won't be able to count them."

**Wow! That's a wonderful promise.
How do you think Abram felt?**

Promised Land

Genesis 12:1–9

God told Abram to move to a new place.
Abram had no map. God said, "I will show
you where to go." Abram started out
walking. He took his wife, nephew, and
servants with him.

When Abram and his family got to a land called Canaan, God said, "This is your new home. I am giving it to you and to everyone who will ever be in your family."

If your parents said, "We're going on a trip, but we can't tell you where," would you trust them to take you to a good place?

Abraham's Visitors

Genesis 17:1–8; 18:1–8

When Abram was 99 years old, God
changed his name to Abraham. His new
name showed that he belonged to God.
Not long after that, three men came by
Abraham's tent, and he invited them
to lunch.

"Quick! Bake some bread," Abraham told his wife. Then Abraham hurried to get some meat cooked. When the food was ready, Abraham brought it to his visitors. The men sat down to eat.

Abraham didn't know it, but his visitors were from heaven.

Sarah Laughs

Genesis 18:9–16

When one of the visitors finished eating, he said, "Where is your wife, Sarah?" "She's over there in the tent," Abraham said. "Next year Sarah will have a baby," the visitor said.

Sarah heard and laughed. She couldn't believe it. *I'm too old to have a baby,* she thought. *Abraham is too old too.*

What if your great-grandmother had a baby? Sarah was that old. Let's see how God keeps His promises.

Baby Isaac

Genesis 21:1–7

In about a year Sarah had a baby boy, just like God had promised. Abraham named the baby Isaac. Isaac means "laughter."

Sarah was so happy with her baby boy.
She said, "God has made me laugh.
Everyone who hears about this will
laugh with me."

God can do anything, but sometimes it takes a while
to see the answer. What would you like to ask Him
to do for you?

A Wife for Isaac

Genesis 24:1–14

Many years later, Isaac was all grown up. "Go back to the land I came from and find a wife for my son," Abraham said to his servant.

The servant loaded up camels with all kinds of wonderful presents. After he got to the land far away, he wasn't sure how to find a wife for Isaac. At a place where girls came to get water, he prayed, "Let the right girl give me water."

How many jugs of water do you think those camels could drink?

Water for the Camels

Genesis 24:15–20

Before the servant had finished praying, a beautiful young woman came to get water. The servant asked her, "Will you give me some water, please?"

44

"Yes," she said. "I'll get water for your camels too." It was a big job. Thirsty camels can drink a lot of water. Back and forth she went, pouring water for them all.

Do you think the man noticed how kind the woman was?

Rebekah

Genesis 24:21–61

The servant knew this woman was the one
to be Isaac's wife. Her name was Rebekah.
The servant took gifts to her family and
asked if Rebekah could marry Isaac.

Her father said she could, and Rebekah wanted to get married too. So she went home with the servant to meet Isaac.

The servant needed God to help him find the right girl.
What do you do when you need God's help?

Isaac and Rebekah

Genesis 24:62–67

The camels swayed and bumped along the road all the way to Canaan where Isaac lived. One evening just before the sun went down, the camels stopped.

A young man was walking in the field. He looked up and saw the camels. His bride had come. Isaac loved Rebekah. He married her.

Do you think Rebekah was excited about being chosen to be Isaac's wife? How do you think she felt about going so far away?

The Twins

Genesis 25:21–26

For many years Rebekah couldn't have babies. So Isaac prayed to God about the problem. God heard Isaac, and He sent *two* babies—twins. When the twins were born, one was all red and fuzzy. Isaac and Rebekah named him Esau.

The other twin had smooth skin. They named him Jacob. Someday, when they were grown up, these boys would be the leaders of two great families.

God has the answers to all our prayers.
What would you like to pray about?

Sneaky Jacob

Genesis 25:27–34

The boys grew up, and one day Esau came in from hunting. Jacob was cooking. "I'm hungry. Give me some of that soup!" said Esau.

Jacob was a sneaky guy. He said, "Give me your rights as the firstborn son, and I will." Esau agreed, "Okay. If I starve, my rights won't help me."

Esau made a bad decision. Pray and ask God to help you make good decisions.

Foolish Esau

Genesis 25:34; 27:1–37

Jacob gave Esau a big bowl of soup, and he ate it. Esau didn't even know he had been tricked.

Later on Esau found out what that bowl of soup cost him. Isaac, their father, gave everything he had to Jacob when it should have been Esau's. Esau had been foolish.

Esau thought he had to have something right now. Why is it foolish *not* to think about consequences?

A Ladder to Heaven

Genesis 27:41–46; 28:10–18

When Esau found out how Jacob had tricked him, he was mad. Jacob was afraid and ran away from him. That night in the desert, Jacob had to sleep outside with a rock under his head for a pillow.

56

He dreamed about a ladder to heaven filled with angels. God spoke to Jacob in the dream and promised to bless him.

What do you think it would be like to have a rock for a pillow?

Rachel

Genesis 29:1–20

Jacob continued his journey, traveling
a long way to his uncle Laban's house.
There he met Laban's beautiful daughter
Rachel. Jacob fell in love with her.

He told Laban, "I'll stay here and work for you if you'll let me marry Rachel." So Jacob stayed and worked seven years for the woman he loved.

Is there anything you'd be willing to wait seven years for?

Tricked!

Genesis 29:21–24

After seven years of hard work, it was finally time for Jacob's wedding. Everyone got dressed. The bride wore a heavy veil over her face. It was so heavy that Jacob couldn't see through it.

Guess what? Laban tricked Jacob. Rachel was not under the veil. It was her sister, Leah, instead.

How do you think Jacob felt when he found out he had been tricked?

Home Again

Genesis 29:25–30; 31:1–55

Jacob was mad at Laban. "What have you done?" Jacob asked. Laban said, "Work some more, and I'll give you Rachel too." Jacob married Rachel and worked seven more years.

Then Jacob decided to leave Rachel's sneaky father. He took his family and everything he had and started back home.

Jacob was going home, but that's where his angry brother, Esau, lived. What do you think happened when they met?

Jacob Wrestles with God

Genesis 32:26–28

When Jacob was almost home, a servant said, "Your brother, Esau, is coming." Jacob thought Esau was coming to hurt him. Jacob was afraid and prayed, "God, save me from my brother!"

That night a man, who was really God, appeared. Jacob wrestled with the man. "Bless me," Jacob said. God blessed Jacob and changed his name to Israel.

Jacob means "sneaky." *Israel* means "one who wrestles with God." Which kind of person would you rather be?

Jacob and Esau Meet

Genesis 33

The next morning Esau came. Jacob bowed in fear in front of him. Surprise! Esau was happy to see Jacob. Esau ran to Jacob and gave him hugs and kisses.

"Who are all these people?" Esau asked. "They are mine," Jacob answered. "God has been good to me." The brothers became friends again.

Do you have brothers and sisters?
Do you treat them kindly?

Joseph's Dreams

Genesis 37:1-8

Jacob had 12 sons. He loved them all, but he loved Joseph best. Joseph liked to tell his brothers about his dreams. He said, in one dream, all 12 brothers had bundles of wheat.

Then he said 11 bundles bowed down to his bundle. Oooo! That made the older brothers mad. "You're not the king over us," they told him.

God had a plan for this family that no one could see yet. God has a plan for your family too.

Joseph's Coat

Genesis 37:3, 12–20

Jacob gave Joseph a beautiful coat with long sleeves. This made his brothers jealous.

One day Jacob said, "Joseph, go check on your brothers." So off Joseph went. His brothers saw him coming. "Here comes the dreamer," they said. "Let's get rid of him." Watch out, Joseph!

Those brothers were up to no good.
What would they do to Joseph?

Joseph Is Sold

Genesis 37:21–28

The brothers hated Joseph. But one of them said, "Let's not hurt him. Let's just throw him down this well." He planned to rescue Joseph later. So they took off Joseph's coat and threw him in.

About that time, some men on camels rode by. "Hey," the brothers said, "let's sell him to be a slave." They sold their own brother.

What the brothers did was awful.
What would happen next?

Joseph the Slave

Genesis 39:1-6

Joseph was not alone. God was watching over him. Soon a rich man named Potiphar bought him to be his slave. Joseph worked and did great at everything Potiphar asked him to do.

So Potiphar put Joseph in charge of his whole house, and everyone had to do what Joseph said.

Even when things look bad, God is watching over His children. He's watching over you right now.

Joseph in Jail

Genesis 39:6–20

Everything was going great for Joseph, until one day Potiphar's wife tried to trick him. She told lies about Joseph, and Potiphar believed her.

Potiphar threw Joseph into jail. Poor Joseph. His brothers sold him, a lady lied about him, and he was thrown into jail. It wasn't fair. But God had a plan for Joseph.

Lots of things happen to us that aren't fair.
But, remember, God always has a plan to help us.

Joseph Explains Dreams

Genesis 40:1–13, 20–21

In the prison, one of the prisoners told Joseph about a dream he'd had. Joseph listened carefully, and God showed him what the man's dream meant.

Joseph said that in three days the man would be working for the king of Egypt like he had before being put in prison. Sure enough, that's exactly what happened.

Joseph knew what God could do. He had learned how to listen to God. You can too.

The Baker's Dream

Genesis 40:16–22

Another prisoner dreamed he had three baskets of bread that he had baked for the king. In his dream the birds kept eating up all the bread.

Joseph didn't have very good news about this dream. He said, "In three days you will die." Joseph told the truth.

Why do you think Joseph was so good at telling what dreams meant? The most important dream Joseph would hear about was just ahead.

The King's Dream

Genesis 41:1–36

One night the king of Egypt dreamed that seven skinny cows came from the river and ate up seven fat cows. No one could figure out what the dream meant.

82

"Call for Joseph," said the first man who had told Joseph his dream in the prison. They did, and God showed Joseph what the king's dream meant. There would be seven years with lots of food. Then there would be seven years with almost no food.

That was a scary dream, wasn't it? Sometimes our dreams mean something, and sometimes they are just dreams.

Joseph in Charge

Genesis 41:37–43

When the king heard what Joseph said, he did something amazing. He put Joseph in charge of gathering enough food to feed everyone during the hungry time.

The king took off his royal ring and put it on Joseph's finger. He gave Joseph fine clothes to wear and put a gold chain around his neck. The king had Joseph ride in one of the royal chariots, and everyone had to bow down to him.

Joseph went from being a prisoner in the morning to a ruler in the afternoon. That was because God had a plan for Joseph and his family.

Joseph's Brothers Visit Egypt

Genesis 41:46–42:6

For the next seven years, Joseph stored lots of food. Then the hungry time came. It was bad for other lands, but the people of Egypt had food.

Joseph's family, back home, were very hungry. "Go to Egypt and buy grain," Jacob told his sons. So ten brothers packed up and went to Egypt. The youngest brother, Benjamin, stayed home.

87

Whoa! What do you think the brothers will do when they see Joseph?

Spies!

Genesis 42:7-20

When the brothers came to the palace,
Joseph knew right away who they were.
But they didn't recognize him.

88

"You're spies," he said to test them. They replied, "No, we've come to buy food." They told Joseph all about their family.

Joseph gave them food but said if they ever came back they must bring their youngest brother.

Joseph wanted to see Benjamin. What do you think the brothers were thinking? Do you think they'll bring Benjamin next time?

The Bowing Brothers

Genesis 43:15–26

One day Joseph's brothers needed more food. They came back to Egypt and brought Benjamin with them. Joseph told his servants to prepare a feast for them.

When Joseph came to the feast, all the brothers bowed down to him. It was just like Joseph's dream about his brothers' bundles of wheat bowing down to his.

Do you think Joseph's dream had come true?

Joseph Tricks His Brothers

Genesis 43:29–44:13

When Joseph saw Benjamin, he was so happy, he began to cry. But he didn't let anyone see his tears. Joseph gave the brothers the grain they wanted.

But he tricked them. He put his cup in Benjamin's sack. The rule was that whoever took something from the ruler had to be his servant forever. Benjamin couldn't go home.

Joseph tricked his brothers because he wanted to see if their hearts had changed or if they would let someone take another brother. What would happen next?

Jacob Goes to Egypt

Genesis 44:3–45:28

The brothers begged Joseph not to keep
Benjamin. Joseph saw that their hearts
had changed. He said, "I am your brother
Joseph. You sold me to be a slave, but
God sent me here to save your lives."

"Hurry, go home and get our father and your families and bring them here." And that's how God's people, the Israelites, came to live in Egypt.

God always has a plan. He has a plan for you too.

A Mean King

Exodus 1:8–14

Years later, long after Joseph died, a mean king made the Israelites his slaves. The slave masters were mean too. They made the Israelites work harder and harder to make bricks and do other things for the king.

"There are too many Israelites, and they are too strong," said the king. So he thought up an awful thing to do.

Why do you think the king was mean to the Israelites?

A Baby Boy

Exodus 1:22–2:2

That mean old king said, "Every time an Israelite baby boy is born, you must throw him into the river." That was terrible!

One day an Israelite woman had a beautiful baby boy. She decided to hide her baby from the evil king and his helpers. It was a good choice.

When we make the right choice, God always helps us.
Let's see what happened next.

The Good Sister

Exodus 2:3–4

After a while the baby's mother couldn't hide him anymore. So she got a basket and fixed it so the water could not get inside.

Then she put the baby into the basket and put the basket into the river. The baby's big sister, Miriam, stayed close by to see what would happen.

Miriam must have been very frightened. What do you think she said when she prayed for her little brother?

A Princess Finds Moses

Exodus 2:5–10

God was watching over the baby. When the princess came to the river to take a bath, she saw the basket. "Go get that basket," she told her servant.

The princess looked inside the basket. Just then the baby cried, and she felt sorry for him. The princess decided to keep him as her son. She named him Moses.

This was exciting! Moses was going to be a prince of Egypt. But something even better was about to happen.

Moses' Real Mother Helps

Exodus 2:7–10

Miriam was still watching. Even though she was frightened, she stepped out and asked, "Do you need someone to take care of the baby?" The princess smiled. "Why, yes," she replied.

Miriam ran home and got her mother—
Moses' own mother—to take care of
him. God saved Baby Moses and gave
him back to his mother for a long time.

**Many exciting things were going to happen to Moses
when he grew up. Let's read on.**

Moses Runs Away

Exodus 2:11–3:3

After a while Moses went to the palace
to live. When he was grown up, Moses did
something very bad. He killed another man.

Moses ran away to live in the desert. He married a lady named Zipporah. Her father's name was Jethro. One day when Moses was out with the sheep, he saw a bush in the desert. It was on fire, but it didn't burn up.

What was going on? Why didn't the bush burn up?

Strange Fire

Exodus 3:4–12

Moses went to look at this strange fire. God spoke to Moses from the fire. "Don't come any closer. Take off your sandals. You are on holy ground." Moses was scared. He covered his face. "Go, bring My people out of Egypt," God said.

"I can't do that," Moses said. But God promised to help Moses lead the people.

Whenever God asks us to do hard things, He will help us. Let's see how He helped Moses.

Moses Goes Home

Exodus 4:14–5:1

Moses went home to Egypt to talk to the Israelites about being free. God sent Moses' brother Aaron to help him.

The Israelites fell right down on their knees and thanked God for remembering them. Then it was time for Moses to go see the mean king. Moses took Aaron with him.

Oh my! Moses had to ask the king to let all those people go free. What do you think the king said?

The King Says No!

Moses walked right up to the king and said, "God says, 'Let My people go!'" The king said, "I don't know your God. Why should I obey Him? These people have work to do. They cannot leave."

112

Then the king made the people work even harder. What a mean man! This made the Israelite leaders angry with Moses.

Do you think Moses had made a mistake?

A Mistake?

Exodus 5:19–6:9

The Israelite leaders were angry. They thought Moses had surely made a big mistake. "You made the king hate us," they said.

Moses talked to God. "Lord, why have You brought this trouble on the people? Is this why You sent me here?" God answered, "You will see what I will do to the king."

Sometimes even when we do good, things get worse for a while. This is when we need to remember that God can see ahead.

The Walking-Stick Miracle

Exodus 7:8–13

God sent Moses and Aaron back to the king. "Let God's people go," Moses said. "Do a miracle," said the king. Aaron threw down his walking stick, and it became a snake.

The king's magicians threw down their
sticks, and they became snakes too.
But Aaron's snake swallowed them all.
God's power was the strongest. Still
the king was so evil and his heart was
so hard that he said, "No, your people
cannot leave."

This is just getting harder and harder.
How will God rescue His people?

A River Turns to Blood

Exodus 7:14–24

God said to Moses, "Go meet the king at the river. Tell him to let My people go, or I will turn this river into blood." Of course, the king said no. So Aaron hit the water with his walking stick, and the river turned to blood.

118

It smelled awful, and there was no water for the people to drink.

Sometimes people don't want to listen to God. What else do you think will happen to that stubborn king?

Frogs, Frogs, Frogs

Exodus 7:25–8:15

After seven days Moses went back to the king. "Let God's people go," said Moses. "No," said the king.

This time God sent frogs. Not just one or two, but more than anyone could count! The frogs went in the houses, in the beds, in the food, and in the ovens. The frogs were icky, and they were everywhere.

God meant business. How much worse do you think it will get before the king says yes?

Gnats, Flies, and Boils

Exodus 8:16–9:12

Every time the king said no, things just went from bad to worse in Egypt. God sent little bitty gnats that crawled all over the people.

Next He sent millions of flies. They were everywhere. Cows got sick and died. Then people got sick with big sores called *boils*. But the king still said no each time.

That king sure was stubborn! Can you guess what awful thing came next?

Hail, Locusts, and Darkness

Exodus 9:13–10:29

Next God sent a storm. Big chunks of ice called *hail* pounded every plant into the ground. Then hungry grasshoppers called *locusts* blew in with the wind. There were so many of them, the people couldn't see the ground. The grasshoppers ate all the food.

Then God sent darkness right in the middle of the day. The Egyptians couldn't see anything. But the king still said no.

Why do you think the king kept saying no?

Standing-Up Dinner

Exodus 11:1–12:28

God told His people to fix a dinner of roast lamb and to eat dinner standing up with all their clothes on.

126

He told them to have their walking
sticks in their hands. God knew the king
would soon change his mind, and His
people needed to be ready to go.

**On this night the children got to stay up late
and eat dinner with their parents.
Tell what you think happened next.**

Something Awful

Exodus 12:29–51

At midnight because the king was so stubborn, something awful happened in Egypt. All the oldest boys, cows, horses, and other animals died. But not one of God's people or their animals died.

128

Finally the king said, "Take everything you have and leave Egypt." God's people were free at last!

God doesn't want bad things to happen to people, but He had to make the king listen.

Cloud and Fire

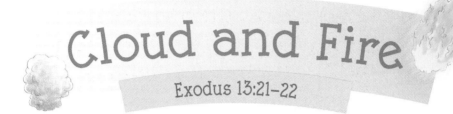

Exodus 13:21–22

When God's people left Egypt, they
marched out into the desert. God did
something very special to help them. He
sent a tall cloud to guide them during
the day.

It was very dark in the desert at night.
So God changed the cloud to fire. It was
like a giant night-light. Now God's people
could travel some during the day and
some at night.

**God loved His people. He was taking care of them
just like He takes care of us.**

Trapped at the Red Sea

Exodus 14:5–14

Back in Egypt the king changed his mind. He sent his army after the Israelites to bring them back. Closer and closer the army of horses and chariots came.

God's people stood right by the Red Sea. There was no way across the water. The king's soldiers were behind them, and the sea was in front of them. It looked as if they were trapped, but they weren't.

**How do you think God's people felt at that moment?
Sad? Scared? Hopeful?**

A Dry Path

Exodus 14:15–31

Just then God moved the tall cloud behind His people to hide them from the enemy. The Egyptians couldn't see anything. The cloud made it dark for them. But it gave light to God's people on the other side of the cloud.

134

Then Moses raised his hand over the sea. All night God pushed back the sea with a strong wind. And the water split to make a dry path to the other side. The Israelites safely reached the other side. But when the Egyptian army tried to use the same path, the water came back together and covered the soldiers. And that was the end of the king's army.

Can you imagine what it was like to walk on a path in the middle of the sea?

Food and Water

Exodus 15:22–17:7

God led His people through the desert. God loved them. He made sure they had plenty of food and water. He gave them a strange, white food called *manna*. It came from the sky and was very good for them, but the people whined and whined.

Once God even made water come out of a rock so they would have fresh water to drink. The people were happy to have water. They stopped whining for a little while.

God wants us to be thankful. What are you thankful for? What should you tell God?

Ten Commandments

Exodus 20:2–17; 24:12–18

One day God called Moses up to the top of a mountain to have a talk.

God gave Moses many rules to help His people know how to live. God wrote the rules on stone with His finger. We call these rules *The Ten Commandments*.

God gives us rules to keep us safe. Rules help us live happy lives. Moms and dads have rules too. Can you name one?

A Tent House for God

Exodus 25:8–9; 31:1–11

God had told Moses to build a Holy Tent so that God could live close to His people. Then God gave Moses someone to help him build the Holy Tent.

The helper's name was Bezalel. God said His Spirit would help Bezalel know how to make beautiful things from silver and gold and jewels and carved wood for God's house.

God gives different skills and talents to different people. What do you do best? Have you thanked God for this special talent?

A Holy Box

Exodus 25:10–22; 40:20–21, 34–38

One of the things Bezalel made for the Tent was the Holy Box. He covered the box with pure gold. He made a lid of pure gold too.

Moses put the stones with God's commandments on them inside the Holy Box. Bezalel and Moses worked hard to make everything perfect. When the Holy Tent was finished, God's presence filled it up. God had come to live with His people.

Where do people go to worship God today?

Moses and Joshua

Exodus 33:7–11

Before the Holy Tent was built, Moses would set up another tent outside the camp. When Moses went to the tent to talk with God, he often took a young man named Joshua with him.

All the people stood outside and watched the two men go by. As soon as Moses and Joshua were inside the tent, the tall cloud would come down and cover the doorway.

What do you suppose was going on inside the tent? Let's see.

Inside the Tent

Exodus 33:11; Joshua 1:1–9

Inside the tent God and Moses talked like old friends, and Joshua listened. This was one of the ways Moses was teaching Joshua how to be a leader of God's people.

146

When Moses left the tent to go home,
Joshua liked to stay at the tent.

It was important for Joshua to get to know God.
God had lots of work for him to do.

You can get to know God, too, by praying and
listening to what God says in the Bible.

Moses Sees God

Exodus 33:18–23; 34:29–35

One day Moses asked God, "Will You show me how great You are?" God tucked Moses into a crack in a rock and passed in front of him.

Moses only saw God's back. But it was enough. Moses' face became so shiny from being close to God that people couldn't look at him. Moses had to cover his face to keep the light from hurting their eyes.

Wow, Moses really got close to God, didn't he?
How do you think we can get close to God?

12 Men Explore

Numbers 13:1–14:35

One day Moses sent 12 men to explore the land God had promised His people. The land had lots of food, but the people who lived there were like giants. Two men, Joshua and Caleb, said, "Don't worry. God is with us, and He is stronger than any giants."

But the other men were afraid and said, "We can't go into the land." God was not happy with His people. They did not trust Him. So God's people had to wander around in the desert 40 more years.

God wants us to believe His Word.
Of the 12 men who explored the new land,
who were the two that trusted God?

151

Balaam's Donkey

Numbers 22:1–22

Close to the end of their time in the desert, all God's people camped near a city. The king of that city was afraid when he saw so many people camped nearby. He sent for a prophet named Balaam. "Do something to make these people go away," he said.

So Balaam started off on his donkey to see what he could do. That made God angry because He wanted His people to be there.

God had a big surprise for Balaam. Turn the page and see what happened.

The Donkey and the Angel

Numbers 22:22–35

God sent an angel with a sword to stop
Balaam. Balaam couldn't see the angel,
but his donkey could. The donkey stopped.
When Balaam beat the donkey to make it
go, the donkey said, "Why are you beating
me?" Then Balaam saw the angel. The
angel told Balaam to help God's people.

**God can do anything. He even made a donkey talk
so Balaam would pay attention.**

Crossing Jordan

Joshua 3

Finally it was time for God's people to go into their new land. But first they had to cross the Jordan River.

There were no bridges or boats. God told the priests to carry the Holy Box and walk into the water. When they did, God made a dry path, and His people walked across to the other side of the river.

What do you think other people thought when they heard what God did for His people?

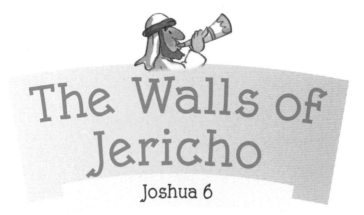

The Walls of Jericho

Joshua 6

The first city they came to was Jericho. It had huge walls and gates and guards everywhere. God said, "March around Jericho every day for six days. Seven priests with trumpets must march at the front."

"On the seventh day, march around seven times. Then have the priests blow one long blast on their trumpets. The people must shout and the walls will fall down." The people obeyed and down came those walls.

Sometimes God asks us to do things we don't understand. We just need to obey.

The Sun Stands Still

Joshua 10:1–14

Joshua fought hard to win the land God had promised to His people. And God helped him. One day God sent huge hailstones to fall on the enemy.

Later that day the battle was not finished. Joshua said, "Sun, stand still!" God kept the sun right where it was until His people won the battle.

**Nothing is impossible when God is on our side.
God wants to help us.**

Deborah

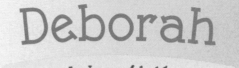

Judges 4:1–16

When the people got settled
in their new land, God
gave them leaders to
help them. One of
them was a woman
named Deborah.
People came to
her under a
tree, so that
she could settle
their arguments.

She and her general, Barak, went into battle. Deborah was a brave woman who could win against their enemies. God was on her side.

Deborah was only one of many brave leaders.
Let's see who else was a leader.

Gideon

Judges 6:11–24

One day an angel came to a man named Gideon. The angel said, "The Lord is with you, mighty warrior! Go save God's people."

164

Gideon said, "Not me. My family is the weakest in our tribe, and I am the weakest in our family." The angel said to Gideon, "I will be with you." And that's how Gideon became a leader of God's people.

God doesn't always look for the strongest person to do His work. He looks for people who will do what He asks them to do.

Too Many Soldiers

Judges 6:33–7:8

Gideon was scared, but he decided he would do what God asked. He got an army together. God said, "You have too many soldiers." Gideon sent thousands of men home. God said, "You still have too many. Take them to drink water. Keep only those who put water in their hands and lap it like a dog." That left Gideon with only 300 soldiers.

How could Gideon win a war with only 300 soldiers? Just see what God does next!

Trumpets and Pots

Judges 7:16–22

God told Gideon to give each of his men trumpets and jars. A burning torch was inside each jar.

While the enemy was sleeping, Gideon's men blew their trumpets as loudly as they could. Then they broke their pots and let the fire from the torches shine. The enemy soldiers woke up, and they were so scared they began fighting one another. After a while they ran away.

Because Gideon did what God told him to do, God won the battle for His people! Yea, God!

Samson

Judges 13:1–5, 24–25

One of the leaders of God's people was chosen before he was born.

An angel told the mother, "You will have a son! But you must never cut his hair. His long hair will show that he's a Nazirite—someone who has work to do for God."

170

This baby grew up to be very strong. His name was Samson, and he always won against his enemies.

It's too bad Samson wasn't as smart as he was strong.
He was about to get in a bunch of big trouble.

Samson's Haircut

Judges 16:4–21

Samson had a girlfriend. Her name was Delilah. She asked, "What makes you so strong, Samson?" At first he wouldn't tell her. She begged and whined. Finally he said, "If someone shaved my head, I would lose my strength."

When Samson fell asleep, Delilah had someone to shave off his hair. Samson wasn't strong anymore. Now his enemies had no trouble taking him to their prison.

Poor Samson. He wasn't wise when he chose Delilah to be his friend. We need to be careful about the kind of friends we choose.

Pushing the Pillars

Judges 16:23–31

In prison Samson's hair grew long again. One night his enemies had a party. They brought Samson in and made fun of him.

Samson asked God to help him once more. And God did. When Samson pushed against the pillars that held up the building, down it all came on top of everyone. Those people would never hurt anyone again.

Samson was the strongest man in the Bible. Who made him strong?

Ruth and Naomi

Ruth 1

Ruth and Naomi were widows. That means their husbands had died. Ruth had been married to Naomi's son. One day Naomi decided to go back to the land from which her family had come.

Ruth decided to go with her. Naomi thought Ruth might miss her family and friends. She told Ruth not to come with her. But Ruth said, "Don't ask me to leave you!" And so they went together.

Ruth didn't know where she was going, and she didn't know the big surprise waiting for her. Try to guess what it was.

Ruth Gathers Grain

Ruth 2

Ruth and Naomi were very poor. They didn't have enough to eat. Naomi was too old to work, so Ruth went out to a rich man's field to gather leftover grain for food. The rich man saw her. She was a beautiful young woman. "Stay here and work in my field," he told her.

Ruth was taking care of Naomi, and God was
taking care of them both. But God wasn't finished
with His surprise yet. What will it be?

179

Ruth and Boaz

Ruth 3–4

Naomi decided Boaz would be a good husband for Ruth. She told Ruth what she should do to see if Boaz wanted to marry her. Ruth did exactly what Naomi said. Boaz liked Ruth and wanted to marry her. So they were married and had a little boy. That made all of them happy.

God's surprises are always very special if we can just wait for His time to give them to us. Tell about a surprise you've had.

Hannah's Prayer

1 Samuel 1:1–18

One day a woman named Hannah went to God's Holy Tent to pray. She asked God for a baby son. She promised God her son would work for Him all his life. Eli, the priest, saw her praying. He thought there was something wrong. Hannah told him she was very sad and talking to God about her troubles. Eli said, "May the Lord give you what you want." Hannah was not sad anymore.

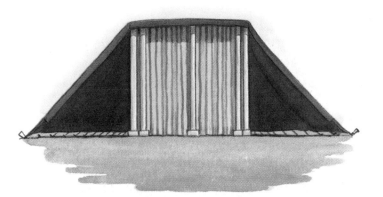

What do you pray to God about?

Hannah's Boy

1 Samuel 1:19–28; 2:19

Hannah's prayer was answered. She had a baby boy and named him Samuel, which means "God heard."

When Samuel was about three years old, Hannah took him to Eli, the priest at the Holy Tent. Hannah loved Samuel very much. Every year she made him a new coat.

Hannah kept her promise to God by taking Samuel to Eli. God had big plans for Samuel. What do you think they were?

Samuel Listens

1 Samuel 3:1–14

Samuel's job was to help Eli in the Lord's work. One night Samuel ran to where Eli the priest was sleeping. Samuel had heard someone call his name, and he thought it was Eli. "I didn't call you," Eli said. "Go back to bed."

So Samuel went back to bed, but the voice called him two more times. After the third time, Eli knew that God was calling Samuel. Eli told Samuel to say, "Speak, Lord. I'm listening." God told Samuel that He was going to punish Eli's sons because they were evil.

What would you do if God called you in the middle of the night?

Losing the Holy Box

1 Samuel 4

When Samuel had grown up,
there was a war. God's people
decided to take the Holy Box
into the battle.
When they did this,
they did not follow God's
rules. Guess what? The enemy
captured the Holy Box of
God and took it home
with them. God's
people were sad.

God's people knew the rules, but
decided not to follow them.
What do you think about following rules?

189

Coming Home

1 Samuel 5–6:13

As soon as the enemy got the Holy
Box of God home, bad things started
happening to them. They wanted to get
rid of it. They put the Holy Box in a cart
pulled by two cows and sent it home.
When God's people saw the Holy Box
coming, they were so happy!

God's people didn't even have to fight to get the
Holy Box back. God will take care of us, even
when someone is mean to us.

191

A Scary Thunderclap

1 Samuel 7:2–11

The enemy wasn't quite through yet.
They saw God's people meeting together
and decided to attack them. The people
begged Samuel to pray. He did, and God
sent a thunderclap so loud it frightened
the enemy soldiers. Then God's people
chased them away.

193

Wow! That must have been quite a thunderclap.
God can even use nature to win over evil.

A King for Israel

1 Samuel 8–15

After a while God's people decided they wanted a king. God didn't think that was a good idea, but He told Samuel to pour oil on the head of a tall, young farmer named Saul. That showed God had chosen him to be king.

At first Saul let Samuel help him make good decisions. But then Saul decided to do things that made God unhappy. So God decided to let someone else be king in Saul's place. It made Samuel sad to tell Saul that God didn't want him to be king anymore.

Isn't it too bad about Saul? Let's see who God chose to be the next king.

The Youngest Son

1 Samuel 16:1–13

God sent Samuel to the house of a man named Jesse to choose a new king. When Samuel looked at seven of Jesse's sons, God said to him, "Don't look at how tall or handsome they are."

"Are these all of your sons?" Samuel asked. Jesse said, "My youngest son is taking care of the sheep. His name is David." God said to Samuel, "David is the one I've chosen."

God doesn't care if you are tall or short or have blue eyes or brown. He just wants you to have a heart that loves Him.

David the Shepherd

1 Samuel 16:11; Psalm 23

David was a shepherd. It was his job to protect and care for sheep. When he was with the sheep, he made up songs and sang them to God. One of those songs says: "The Lord is my shepherd. I have everything that I need."

As David watched the sheep, he became close friends with God.

It's good to sing songs to God.
What is your favorite song to sing to Him?

David and the Giant

1 Samuel 17:1–24

God's Holy Spirit came to be with David. It made him brave and strong. One day Jesse told David to go check on his brothers who were soldiers. When David got to the battlefield, he found the soldiers were all afraid of a giant named Goliath. Goliath liked to yell at the soldiers and scare them. He wanted to hurt them.

God gave David courage so he wouldn't be afraid of the giant. What would you do if you needed some courage?

Down Goes the Giant

1 Samuel 17:25–58

David wasn't afraid of Goliath. He gathered five smooth small stones and put them in his pouch. Then with his slingshot in one hand, David went to meet Goliath.

The giant laughed when he saw that David was just a boy. But David shot a stone from the slingshot. It hit Goliath in the head and killed him.

David was brave, and he trusted God.
God will help us in scary times if we just ask Him.

King Saul Chases David

1 Samuel 18–23

By killing the giant Goliath, David became a hero. God's people loved him. King Saul became jealous of David and eventually tried to kill him. Saul and his soldiers chased after David and hunted for him everywhere.

But David and the brave men who went
with him were protected by God, and
Saul couldn't catch them.

Let's see how David gets away from Saul.
You may be surprised.

David and Jonathan

1 Samuel 18:1–4; 20

King Saul had a son named Jonathan.
Jonathan was a prince. He and David
were best friends. He even gave David
his coat. Jonathan knew his father
wanted to hurt David. So Jonathan
helped David run away and hide from
Saul. That was a brave thing for Prince
Jonathan to do. If David became the
next king, Jonathan would never be
king of Israel.

Best friends help each other. Do you have a best friend? What could you do to help your friend?

Jonathan's Son

1 Samuel 31; 2 Samuel 1:1–11; 5:1–4; 9

One day King Saul and his son Jonathan died in a battle against the enemy. When David heard this, he was very sad. Soon afterward, David became king. He always took care of his best friend Jonathan's son Mephibosheth. Mephibosheth was crippled in both feet.

David loved God and wanted to please Him.
But one time David made a big mistake.
Let's see what happened.

David Does Wrong

2 Samuel 11–12:13; Psalm 51

David usually went to war with his soldiers. But one time he stayed home and got into big trouble. He took another man's wife as his own. The woman's name was Bathsheba. Then David sent the man into battle to be killed. That was wrong!

When David realized how wrong he had been, he was truly sorry. He asked God to forgive him, and God did.

God will forgive us if we are truly sorry for what we've done wrong and ask His forgiveness.

A Wise Woman

2 Samuel 20:1, 14–22

Joab, David's general, and the army were trying to catch a troublemaker. They were digging under the wall of a city to make it fall down. Then a wise woman inside the city called down to Joab, "What are you doing?"

"We're trying to capture a troublemaker," Joab said. The wise woman told the city leaders that there was a troublemaker hiding in their city. So the leaders captured and killed the bad man. When Joab heard this, he took his army and went home. The city was saved.

We don't even know this lady's name, but we remember her because she was brave.

The Wisest Man

1 Kings 3:4–15

David was king for forty years.
He had many sons. But it was
his son Solomon who became
king when David died.
Solomon knew that wise
kings make good decisions.
He prayed and asked God to make him
wise so that he could understand
God's laws. God heard his prayer
and made him the wisest man who
ever lived.

Any one of us can ask God to make us wise, and He will. Let's see how Solomon's wisdom helped two women.

Whose Baby?

1 Kings 3:16–28

Two women brought a baby to Solomon.
Each woman said the baby was hers.
Solomon knew just what to do to find
out who the real mother was. He said he
could cut the baby in half and give one
part to each woman.

But one woman pointed to the other woman and said, "No, don't hurt the baby. Give the baby to her." Then Solomon knew the woman who said this was the real mother.

Solomon wasn't really going to hurt the baby. What was he trying to find out?

Two Kingdoms

1 Kings 12:20; 16:29–33; 17:1

After Samuel, David, and Solomon died, God's people were split into two kingdoms—Israel in the north and Judah in the south. King Ahab ruled Israel. He did many things that God said were wrong. He worshiped idols and did more evil than any of the kings before him.

So God sent Elijah, the prophet, to teach Ahab a lesson. Elijah told Ahab that there would be no rain for many years. This made Ahab very angry.

Ahab and his wife, Jezebel, wanted to kill Elijah. But God wanted him to live. Let's see how God protected Elijah.

Elijah Runs Away from King Ahab

1 Kings 17:7–15

Elijah had to run away from Ahab and camp near a brook. God sent birds to bring the prophet food.

When the brook dried up, God told Elijah
to go ask a certain woman for food.
"I only have enough left for one meal
for me and my son," she said. Elijah
said, "Cook for me first, and you'll be all
right." So she did.

The woman believed what Elijah said,
and guess what? After she fed Elijah,
she never ran out of food.

Whose God Is Real?

1 Kings 18:1, 15–24

Three years passed with no rain. Finally, God told Elijah to go meet King Ahab. "There you are, you big troublemaker," said the king. But it was really the king who had caused the trouble.

"Let's see whose god is real," Elijah said. So the king's prophets built one altar to their god, and Elijah built an altar to his God. They put offerings on each of them. Then they prayed and waited to see whose god would answer their prayers by sending fire to burn up the sacrifice.

What do you suppose Elijah was up to?

Fire from Heaven

1 Kings 18:25–46

The king's prophets screamed at their fake gods to send fire. No fire came. Elijah teased, "Pray louder." They did. But nothing happened. When they stopped, Elijah had water poured over everything on the altar he'd built. Then he prayed to God in heaven to send fire.

Fire came down. It burned up the offering, the stones, and the water. Then the people knew Elijah's God was the most powerful.

When Elijah prayed again, it began to rain. How do you think the king felt about that?

Elijah in the Desert

1 Kings 19:1–8

Even though rain had come, King Ahab and his evil wife, Jezebel, still wanted to kill Elijah. Elijah ran for his life to the desert. He was so tired he lay right down and went to sleep.

Soon someone tapped him on the shoulder. An angel had come to make Elijah dinner. The angel fed Elijah a second time too. Then Elijah was strong enough to make a long journey.

What do you suppose Elijah thought when an angel brought him food?

God Speaks to Elijah

1 Kings 19:9–18

Elijah was still being chased by the evil king, and that made Elijah sad. Elijah went into a cave. God said, "Stand here and I will pass by." A strong wind blew, but God didn't speak. An earthquake shook the ground, but God didn't speak.

A fire burned, but still God didn't speak. Then when it was quiet, Elijah heard the gentle voice of God. "Go find a man named Elisha. He will be a helper to you, and he will be the next prophet."

229

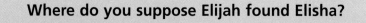

Elijah's Helper

1 Kings 19:19–21

Elijah left the desert right away. He found Elisha plowing a field. Elijah put his coat over the young man. That meant he wanted Elisha to be his helper. First Elisha and his family had a big feast. Then he said good-bye to his mother and father and followed Elijah.

Elijah did exactly what God told him to do. Now he and Elisha would work for God together.

A Bad Queen

1 Kings 21–22:39

King Ahab and his evil wife, Jezebel, decided they wanted a neighbor's land. Speaking badly against God or the king was against the law. Jezebel got some people to lie and say the neighbor, Naboth, had said bad things about both God and King Ahab.

So Jezebel had Naboth killed, and King Ahab took Naboth's land. Not long afterward King Ahab and his wife both died terrible deaths.

God saw what Ahab and Jezebel had done. How do you think that made God feel?

Chariot of Fire

2 Kings 2:1–12

Elijah was getting old. His helper, Elisha, went with him everywhere.

One day Elijah and Elisha were together when God sent a chariot and horses made of fire. The fiery horses and chariot came between Elijah and Elisha. Then *whoosh!* All of a sudden Elijah went up to heaven in a whirlwind. Elisha saw him go.

Someday we will go to heaven. It will be a wonderful place. Who do you think we'll see there?

Elijah's Coat

2 Kings 2:13–14

As the whirlwind took Elijah to heaven, his coat fell off and landed on the ground. Elisha picked it up.

He went to the river and hit the water with the coat. He said, "Where is the God of Elijah?" Elisha wanted to see if God's power was on him like it had been on Elijah. It was. The water split in the middle, and Elisha walked across on dry ground.

This was the first miracle God did through Elisha. Keep reading to learn about more miracles that came later.

The Miracle of the Pot of Oil

2 Kings 4:1–7

"My dead husband owed money to a man. That man is going to make my two sons his slaves," a woman told Elisha. "I have nothing but this small pot of oil."

238

"Get empty jars from your neighbors," said Elisha. "Now pour oil into them." When the woman started pouring oil from her pot, it just kept coming. She filled every jar in the house. Then she sold the oil, paid her debt to the man, and saved her boys from slavery.

How could a small pot of oil fill so many big jars and pots? It was a miracle!

Elisha Helps a Little Boy

2 Kings 4:8–37

Another woman also begged Elisha for help. Her little boy had died. Elisha went to her house.

He went to the room where the little boy's body lay and prayed over him. The little boy sneezed and opened his eyes. He had come back to life, and he was just fine.

This was another wonderful miracle.
Only God can give people life.

Poison in the Stew

2 Kings 4:38-41

Elisha met some hungry men. He had his servant make them stew. One of the men wanted to help. He found some plants and added them to the stew. He didn't know they were poisonous.

When the men started eating, they cried, "There's death in the pot!" Elisha put flour into the stew, and the food became safe to eat.

Throwing flour into a stew doesn't usually remove poison. This was another miracle from God.

Food for Everyone

2 Kings 4:42–44

People all over Israel were running out of food. They were hungry. One man brought 20 loaves of bread to Elisha. Elisha said, "Feed the people." The man said, "We can't feed 100 men with so little bread."

Elisha told him to start feeding them and there would be bread left over. Sure enough, that's what happened!

Elisha was not doing these miracles in his own power. God was helping him. What miracle do you think happened next?

Seven Dips in the Jordan River

2 Kings 5:1–14

Naaman, an important soldier, had a terrible skin disease called *leprosy*. People who had leprosy could not come close to other people. They had to live in lepers' towns. Naaman's wife's servant girl said, "I wish my master could meet Elisha. He would heal him."

So Naaman went to find Elisha. "Wash in the Jordan River seven times, and you'll be healed," Elisha said. Naaman was embarrassed. What Elijah told him to do seemed silly. But he went to the river to wash himself, and on the seventh time the leprosy disappeared.

If a dip in the river would make you well from a terrible sickness, would you do it, even if it seemed silly?

A Floating Ax

2 Kings 6:1–7

Some men were building a meeting house for Elisha. As they were chopping down trees for the house, an ax broke. The metal part fell into the river and sank. The man who was using it yelled, "That was an ax I'd borrowed!"

Elisha threw a stick into the water, and the iron ax head floated up.

Wow! Ax heads are heavy and can't float, unless
God makes them do it. God can do anything!

No Food!

2 Kings 6:24–25; 7:1–9

An army surrounded the city of
Samaria, and no one could go in or come
out. The people in the city had no food.
God told Elisha to say that tomorrow
there would be lots of food. About that
time four men decided to see if the
enemy would give them something to
eat. When they got to the camp, there
was no one there.

The soldiers had run away, leaving all their food and gold and clothes. At first the men started to hide the treasure for themselves. But then they decided to share. They told the people in the city, and soon everyone had enough to eat. It was just as Elisha said it would be.

Those four men were not selfish. They could have kept everything they found for themselves, but they didn't. What do you think God wanted them to do?

The Baby Prince

2 Kings 11:1–12:2

Joash was a baby prince. His grandmother was evil. She wanted to kill him so she could be queen. Joash's aunt hid him in God's house until he was seven years old.

252

Then soldiers came to God's house and got him. They made him king even though he was just a little boy. Joash ruled for 40 years in Jerusalem. He did what God said was right.

If you were made king today, what would you do first?

The Sun Goes Backward

2 Kings 20:1–11; Isaiah 38

Hezekiah was a good king. One day he got very sick. He knew he was going to die. He prayed and asked God to let him live a little longer. Then, to be sure that God had heard him, Hezekiah asked for the sun to go backward. He asked for the shadow that was at the bottom of the steps to go back up ten steps. And just as he asked, the shadow moved back up ten steps. And Hezekiah lived 15 more years.

For the sun to move backward would be as amazing as falling up instead of down. It was a miracle!

Captured!

2 Kings 24:18–25:21; 2 Chronicles 36:15–23

Over and over God had warned His people not to worship idols. But they kept right on doing what God had told them not to do. So finally God let an enemy capture His people and take them from the land He'd given them. They were taken far away to a place called Babylon. It was a sad day.

God wants us to do what is right, and He is very
patient. But if we continue to do wrong, we will
have to suffer the consequences.

Beautiful Queen Esther

Esther 1–3

Years later the Persian kingdom defeated Babylon. But God's people were still living in the land of Babylon. One of them was a young woman named Esther.

The king of Persia wanted a beautiful young woman to be his queen. He picked Esther. Soon afterward one of the king's men decided to get rid of all God's people in the kingdom. Since Esther was one of them, it meant he would get rid of her too.

It must have been a very scary time for Esther. What do you think she did?

Esther Saves Her People

Esther 4–9

Esther knew it was up to her to save her people. She also knew that if she visited the king and he got angry, she wouldn't be queen anymore. The king could even have her killed. What should she do?

Esther decided to go to the king anyway. When she went, the king granted her wish that her people would be allowed to live.

Esther was very brave. She did what God wanted her to do, and because she was brave, she saved her people. Yea, Esther!

An Honest Man

Job 1:1–12

Job was an honest man who loved God.
He had a big family and was very rich.
Everything he did pleased God.

262

Then Satan, the enemy of God and man, went to God and said, "You are protecting Job from anything going wrong. That's why he obeys You." "All right," said God. "You can do anything to him except take his life."

Satan is very real. He doesn't like God, and he doesn't like us. But Job was about to find out that God is always with us.

When Bad Things Happen

Job 1:13–2:10

Awful things began to happen to Job.
His children died. His house fell down.
He got sores all over his body.

His cattle were taken away by robbers. His friends told him to turn away from God.

But Job never doubted that God loved him. Job was faithful to God, even in hard times.

When bad things happen, it doesn't mean God has forgotten about us. He's never far away in the bad times. And He wants us to continue to love and obey Him.

A Time for Everything

There is a time for everything that happens in our lives. There are happy times and there are sad times.

There are times when we cry and times
when we laugh.

There are times to hug and times not to
hug.

There is a time to be silent and a time
to speak.

267

**A little bit of everything happens in our lives.
The important thing is to stay close to
God all the time.**

A Message for King Ahaz

Isaiah 7:1–17; 9:2–7

God told the prophet Isaiah to take a message to a king named Ahaz. King Ahaz was in the family of King David. Isaiah told the king that someday God was going to send a child who would grow up to be a leader of all of God's people. He said that this person would be the Prince of Peace and would rule as King forever.

269

Who was Isaiah talking about? Today we know
he was talking about Jesus, God's Son.

Three Brave Men

Daniel 3:1–23

Remember how God's people were captured and taken away to the country of Babylon? The king of that country was Nebuchadnezzar. Three of these young men—Shadrach, Meshach, and Abednego—worked for King Nebuchadnezzar.

But when the king wanted them to bow down and worship a golden idol, they wouldn't do it. So the king told his soldiers to put all three men into a red-hot furnace.

God was pleased that these young men loved Him so much they would not worship the king's idol. What do you think happened next?

The Extra Man

Daniel 3:24–30

Guess what? The men in the furnace didn't burn up. God sent someone to protect them in the furnace. The king was surprised when he saw four people walking around. He told Shadrach, Meshach, and Abednego to come out of the furnace.

Then the king made a new law. It said that no one could say anything bad about the God of these men.

**God has promised to be with us
no matter what happens to us.**

Writing on the Wall

Daniel 5:1–26

Daniel was one of God's people who was a slave in Babylon. One night the new king of Babylon gave a banquet. Suddenly a hand appeared and began writing on the wall something that no one could read. It was very scary!

The king asked Daniel to come and tell him what it meant. Daniel said it meant that God was angry with the king. And the kingdom of Babylon would be divided and given to two other countries, the Medes and Persians.

Daniel always lived for God no matter what anyone said. Let's see what happened to him.

Daniel Disobeys the King

Daniel 6:1–10

Daniel prayed three times every day. Some men in the new kingdom of the Medes and Persians wanted to get rid of Daniel. So they had the new king make a rule that people could only pray to the king. If someone broke the rule, he would be thrown into the lions' den.

But Daniel went to his house and got down on his knees and prayed to God just as he had always done.

Daniel knew that praying to God was more important than obeying the king's new rule.

A Den of Hungry Lions

Daniel 6:11–28

The men caught Daniel praying to God and told the king. The king was sad because he liked Daniel, but the king couldn't change the law. So Daniel was thrown into a den of hungry lions.

But wait! God sent an angel to close the mouths of the lions so they couldn't bite.

In the morning, the king came to see if God had saved Daniel, and sure enough, Daniel was just fine.

God saved Daniel. After being saved from the lions, do you think Daniel went on praying to God three times a day?

Jonah Runs Away

Jonah 1:1–3

"Go to Nineveh," God told a man named Jonah. "Tell them to stop their evil ways." Jonah got up, but he didn't go to Nineveh. He didn't like the people of that city, so he ran away.

Jonah went to the seashore. He got on a ship going the opposite direction from Nineveh. God saw what Jonah was doing.

God always sees what we are doing.
He wants us to make good choices.

A Big Storm!

Jonah 1:4–6

Jonah sailed away on the ship. When the ship was at sea, God sent a big storm. Waves pounded the ship. The sailors were very frightened of the storm.

The captain went down into the bottom
of the ship and found Jonah sleeping.
"Get up and pray to your God too," he
said. "Maybe your God will save us!"

**The captain and everyone prayed.
They knew they needed help from somebody
bigger than themselves.**

Jonah Goes Overboard

Jonah 1:7–16

"Somebody has done something to cause this storm. Let's find out who it is," the sailors said. They decided the storm was Jonah's fault. "You're right. I ran away from God," Jonah told them. "Throw me into the sea. Then it will calm down."

So the sailors tossed Jonah overboard. As soon as Jonah was in the water, the sea became calm.

You might think that would be the end of Jonah, but it wasn't!

Inside a Big Fish!

Jonah 1:17–2:9

Down, down into the swirling water went Jonah. Then *gulp!* Something swallowed him. Jonah was in the stomach of a big fish. God left him there to learn something important. It took three days and three nights.

Then Jonah prayed to God for help. He decided to do what God had told him to do.

It took a while for Jonah to catch on that he needed to obey God. Now, how was he going to get out of that fish?

Jonah Obeys God

Jonah 2:10–3:10

God had a plan. He spoke to that fish.
It swam up close to the beach and spit
Jonah out of its stomach onto dry land.

Right away God said to Jonah, "Get up and go to the great city of Nineveh. Say what I tell you to say." This time Jonah didn't argue. He obeyed. He jumped up and went straight to Nineveh.

Every time we disobey, we get in trouble.
What would be a better choice?

New Testament

An Angel's Message

Luke 1:5–20

A priest named Zachariah went to God's house to burn an incense offering. As soon as he was inside, the angel Gabriel appeared. "Zachariah, you and your wife, Elizabeth, will have a son. You will name him John," Gabriel said.

Zachariah didn't believe it was possible for Elizabeth and him to have a son. They were too old. "Because you don't believe me, Zachariah, you will not be able to talk until the baby is born," Gabriel said.

John was going to be a very important person. He would tell others to get ready because Jesus was coming.

A Baby Named John

Luke 1:57–66

Just as the angel Gabriel had said, a baby boy was born to Zachariah and his wife, Elizabeth.

Their friends were very happy for them.
"Name him Zachariah after his father,"
they said. Zachariah still couldn't talk,
so he wrote down, "His name is John." As
soon as Zachariah wrote that, he could
talk again.

**People don't get to see angels very often,
but when they do, they need to pay attention.
Angels bring messages from God. What is
another way God sends messages?**

Mary's Big Surprise

Luke 1:26–38

Not long after his visit to Zachariah, the angel Gabriel went to see a young woman named Mary. She was a cousin to Elizabeth, Zachariah's wife. Mary lived in Nazareth and was engaged to marry Joseph, the carpenter.

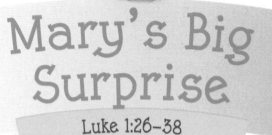

"Don't be afraid, Mary," the angel said. "God is pleased with you. You will have a baby and will name Him Jesus. He will be called the Son of God." This was a big surprise to Mary.

What would you do if an angel suddenly appeared right here in front of you?

Joseph Marries Mary

Matthew 1:18–25

When Joseph heard the news that Mary was going to have a baby, he didn't know what to think. He wasn't married to her yet. God loved Joseph and wanted him to understand that the baby was from God and everything was going to be all right.

So God sent an angel to talk to Joseph in a dream. This angel told Joseph, "Name the baby Jesus. He will save people from their sins." When Joseph heard God's plan, he married Mary.

The name *Jesus* means "savior."
What does a savior do?

God's Baby Son

Luke 2:1-7

The ruler of the land, Augustus Caesar, made a new law to count all the people. Everyone had to register in their hometown. So Joseph and Mary went to their hometown, Bethlehem. The town was full of people. There was no place for Mary and Joseph to sleep.

Finally, Joseph found a place for them where the animals were kept. And that's where God's Baby Son was born. His first bed was on the hay in the box where the animals were fed.

Why do you think God would want His Son to be born where the animals were kept?

Some Sleepy Shepherds

Luke 2:8–12

That night, out in the fields, sleepy shepherds were taking care of their sheep. Suddenly an angel appeared in the sky. The angel's light was so bright, it hurt their eyes.

"Don't be afraid," the angel said. "I have good news for you. A baby was born in Bethlehem town tonight. He is your Savior. You will find Him lying in a feeding box."

303

Who was the first to hear about Baby Jesus?

What the Shepherds Saw

Luke 2:13–20

Then the whole sky filled up with so many angels no one could count them all. They sang, "Glory to God in heaven!" And then, when the song was over, the angels disappeared.

The shepherds hurried to Bethlehem. They found Mary and Joseph and saw Baby Jesus lying in the hay in the feeding box. The shepherds told them everything the angels had said about the child.

If you had been out there on the hill with the shepherds, what would you have been thinking when the angels left?

Gifts for Baby Jesus

Matthew 2:1–12

Soon many of the people who came to register in Bethlehem went home. Mary and Joseph moved into a house.

One day they had visitors who came from far away in the east. These visitors were wise men. They had followed a bright star to find little Jesus. They bowed down and worshiped God's only Son and gave Him expensive presents of gold, frankincense, and myrrh.

Why do you think the wise men came to see little Jesus?

Another Journey

Matthew 2:13–15

After the wise men left, God sent
another angel to Joseph in a dream.
"Take the child and Mary and go to
Egypt," the angel said. "King Herod
wants to kill Jesus. Stay in Egypt until
I tell you it's safe to come home."

It was still night, but Joseph got up out of bed and took Mary and Jesus and headed for Egypt.

Joseph obeyed God immediately. And God kept his family safe. Why is it good to obey quickly?

Home at Last!

Matthew 2:19–23

Mary, Joseph, and Jesus stayed in Egypt until God sent another angel to Joseph in a dream. "Get up and take Mary and Jesus and go home," said the angel. King Herod had died. He could never hurt them again. God and His angels had kept Mary, Joseph, and Jesus safe.

So with happy hearts, they went home to live in Nazareth.

Whew! It was finally safe to go home. How do you think Mary and Joseph felt about that?

Where Is Jesus?

Luke 2:41–45

Every year Jesus' parents went to
Jerusalem to celebrate the Passover.
When Jesus was 12, they went as usual.
When Mary and Joseph started home, they
didn't see Jesus, but it was okay. They
thought Jesus was traveling with friends.

Late in the day they realized He wasn't with any of their friends. Mary and Joseph were very worried and hurried back to Jerusalem, looking for Him all along the way. They were afraid they had lost Jesus.

What are some places where Mary and Joseph might have looked for Jesus?

Jesus with the Temple Teachers

Luke 2:46–50

When Mary and Joseph found Jesus, He was in the Temple—a place where God's people went to worship. Twelve-year-old Jesus was talking with some teachers just like He was one of them. He asked them questions, and He answered theirs.

His mother had a question too. "Son, why did You stay behind? We were worried about You." Jesus said, "You should have known I must be where My Father's work is!"

That was a strange thing for Jesus to say. What do you think He meant?

The Man Who Ate Locusts

Matthew 3:1–13; Mark 1:4–9

Jesus' cousin, John, became a preacher when he grew up. He lived in the desert and wore rough clothes and ate locusts and honey. (Locusts were like grasshoppers.) John told the people to change their hearts and lives and ask forgiveness for their wrongs because Jesus was coming soon.

One day when Jesus was grown up, too, He came to the place where John was preaching and baptizing people. Jesus asked John to baptize Him in the river.

When Jesus asked John to baptize Him, do you think John did it?

John Baptizes Jesus

Matthew 3:13–17

At first John didn't want to baptize Jesus. He thought Jesus should be the one to baptize *him*. But when Jesus said it needed to be this way, John obeyed and took Jesus into the river and baptized Him.

As Jesus came up out of the water, God's Spirit, like a dove, came down to Him from heaven. God spoke and said, "This is My Son, and I love Him. I am very pleased with Him."

Jesus set a good example for us by following God's command to be baptized. Have you been baptized?

Jesus Tempted by Satan

Matthew 4:1–4

Soon God's Spirit led Jesus away from the river and into the desert. Jesus wanted to pray and think about what God wanted Him to do next. Jesus fasted—that means He didn't eat, so He got very hungry. Then the devil, Satan, appeared. Satan knew that Jesus was tired and hungry.

"Turn these rocks into bread," Satan told Jesus. Jesus knew that Satan was trying to get Him to do something wrong. Jesus had studied God's Word, so He remembered what He had learned from the Scriptures. He said, "A person does not live only by eating bread. A person lives by doing everything the Lord says."

Satan doesn't stop picking on people with just one try. He was not through with Jesus yet. Keep reading to see what happened next.

On Top of the Temple

Matthew 4:5–7

Satan took Jesus to Jerusalem and stood Him on the very top of the Temple. The Temple is where God's people worshiped. "If you are God's Son, jump down from this high place," Satan said. "It is written in the Scriptures that God's angels will catch You." That was not a smart thing for Satan to suggest, and Jesus knew it. He answered by saying, "It is also written in the Scriptures, 'Do not test God.'"

It is foolish to test or tease God. Testing God means doing very risky things that might get you hurt.

The Kingdoms of the World

Matthew 4:8–11

That sneaky devil, Satan, had one more test up his sleeve. He took Jesus to a high mountain and showed Him all the kingdoms of the world. Satan said, "Bow down and give honor to me, and I will give You all these things."

Jesus had an answer ready, "Go away from Me! It is written in the Scriptures, 'You must worship only the Lord God.'" So Satan went away.

Even though we can't see Satan, he tries to get us to do things that are wrong. What are some of the things Satan tries to get us to do?

Jesus Heals a Sick Boy

John 4:46–51

Jesus loved little children, and whenever He could, He helped them. One day an important man begged Jesus to come to his house and heal his sick son. But Jesus didn't go. Instead He said, "Go home. Your son will live."

326

The man believed Jesus and went home, but before he got there his servants met him and said, "Your son is well."

When we believe and trust someone to do something we cannot see, that is called *faith*. The man in this story trusted Jesus to keep a promise. Whom do you trust?

Jesus Brings a Girl Back to Life

Mark 5:22–43

Jesus also helped a little girl. Her father's name was Jairus, and he was an important man. "My little daughter is dying," Jairus said. "Please come and pray for her so she will get well and live." Before Jesus could go to the little girl, she died. But Jesus went anyway. With the child's mother and father and three of His followers, Jesus went in the girl's room and took her hand in His. "Little girl," Jesus said, "stand up!" And she did. She was well.

When we ask God for something, sometimes He says yes, and sometimes He says no. The most important thing is that He always hears us.

A Little Boy Helps Jesus

John 6:1-13

Great crowds of people followed Jesus
to see His miracles and hear Him teach
about God's love for them. The people
sometimes forgot to take food with
them. One day a huge crowd of 5,000 men
and their families followed Jesus. It was
late in the day when they reached Jesus,
and the people were getting hungry.

The only one with any food was a little boy with five small loaves of bread and two fish. Jesus blessed the food. His closest followers and helpers gave it to the people. After everyone had plenty to eat, the helpers gathered up 12 baskets of leftover food.

**What do you have that you could give Jesus?
An offering? Some time to help someone?**

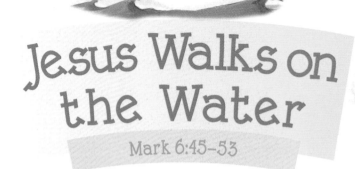

Jesus Walks on the Water

Mark 6:45–53

Later that day Jesus told the followers who were His helpers to go to another city across the lake. He would come after a while. The helpers got into a boat. But that night in the middle of the lake, a strong wind came up. And the men had to work very hard to row the boat.

Then they saw something that frightened them more than the storm. They thought it was a ghost. But it wasn't a ghost. It was Jesus walking on the water. Jesus called to His helpers, "Don't be afraid." Then Jesus got into the boat, and the wind became calm.

If you had been in that boat, what would you have done?

Jesus Loves Children

Luke 18:15–17

Many people wanted to see Jesus. When Jesus saw how sick and sad they were, He wanted to help them. One day some people brought their children to Him. His helpers tried to send them away. Jesus said, "Let the little children come to Me. Don't stop them. You must love and accept God like a little child if you want to enter heaven."

335

If you were one of the children who got to sit on Jesus' lap, what would you say to Him?

A Very Short Man

Luke 19:1–10

Everywhere Jesus went,
there were crowds of
people. In one crowd there
was a very short man named
Zacchaeus. He wanted to
see Jesus, but he couldn't
see over the crowd. So he
climbed a tree.

Jesus said, "Zacchaeus, come down so we can go to your house today." Zacchaeus hurried down and took Jesus to his home. Zacchaeus wanted to do good things. He told Jesus that he'd give half of his money to the poor.

Wouldn't it be exciting to have Jesus come to your house? What would you do if Jesus came to see you?

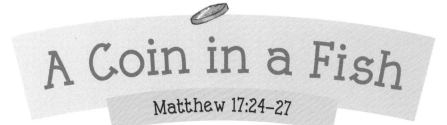

A Coin in a Fish

Matthew 17:24–27

Peter, one of Jesus' helpers, came to tell Jesus it was time for Him to pay taxes. But Jesus and Peter didn't have any money. Jesus knew just what to do. Jesus told Peter, "Go to the lake and catch a fish. You will find a coin in its mouth. Use that coin to pay our taxes."

Aren't you glad Jesus always knows the best thing to do? Talk to Him about your problems.

A Blind Man Sees Again

Mark 10:46–52

Sick people followed Jesus everywhere. They wanted Him to heal them. One man who was blind heard that Jesus was walking by. He cried out, "Jesus, please help me!" People told the man to be quiet, but Jesus asked the man, "What would you like Me to do for you?"

The man said, "I want to see again." So Jesus healed the man's eyes. How happy the man was to see again!

Do you know someone who is sick? You could pray right now and ask Jesus to make them well.

A Very Poor Woman

Mark 12:41–44

Jesus was watching people put their money into the collection box at the Temple where God's people worshiped. Some rich people were very proud as they put in a lot of money.

Then a very poor woman came. In went her two small coins. *Plunk! Plunk!* Jesus told His closest followers, "This woman gave more than the rich people with many coins. The rich people gave only what they did not need, but this poor woman gave all the money she had."

Why do you think the woman gave God all the money she had?

Jesus Stops a Storm

Mark 4:35–41

Jesus and His followers got into a boat and set out across the lake. Jesus was so tired that He fell asleep. Soon a strong wind began to blow. Waves came over the side of the boat. Everyone was very frightened.

They woke Jesus. "Help us, or we'll drown!" Jesus commanded the wind and waves to be still. The wind stopped, and there were no more waves coming into the boat. The lake became calm.

When you are frightened, what do you do?
Remember, Jesus is always there with you.
Just ask Him to help you. He will.

One Lost Sheep

Luke 15:3–7

Here is a story Jesus told. A man had 100 sheep, but he lost one. Now, what was he going to do? He left his 99 sheep safe at home and went looking for the one lost sheep.

He searched everywhere, and when he finally found the lost sheep, he was so happy. He put the sheep on his shoulders and carried it home.

How is Jesus like that shepherd looking for his one lost sheep? Remember, you are as important to Jesus as that one lost sheep was to the shepherd.

A Son Spends All His Money

Luke 15:11-13

Jesus told another story. A man had two sons. The younger son said, "Give me my share of the property and money." So the father divided the property and money between his younger son and older son.

The younger man went to another country far away. He had lots of fun spending every bit of his money.

Do you think the younger son was making a good decision? How do you think his father felt?

The Man Who Ate Pig Food

Luke 15:14–19

After the younger son's money was gone, he got very hungry. A man gave him a job feeding pigs. As the son fed the pigs, he was so hungry that he ate the pig food.

After a while he began to realize he had been very foolish. He said to himself, "My father's servants have plenty of food. I'm going home. I'll tell my father that I have done wrong. I'll ask him if I can just be a servant."

Wow, what a mess! What were some of the choices the son made that got him into a pigpen?

Going Home to Father

Luke 15:20–32

The younger son went home. He was
worried that his father wouldn't want
him. But his father had been looking for
him every day for a long time.

When he saw his son, the father ran to meet him. He hugged him and gave him new clothes. He had a party to welcome him home. He told everyone, "My son was lost, but now he is found!"

The father in this story is like God. God sees us make bad choices, and He is sad. But He is always waiting for us to come back to Him.

Jesus' Best Friends

Luke 10:38–42

One day Jesus went to visit some best friends named Mary, Martha, and Lazarus. Martha was busy getting the meal ready. Mary was sitting and listening to Jesus talk.

Martha became angry and complained, "Jesus, don't You care that Mary left me to do all this work alone? Tell her to help me." Jesus said, "What Mary is learning from Me can never be taken away from her."

Why was Martha angry? What did Jesus tell her?

Jesus Brings Lazarus Back to Life

John 11:1–44

One day Lazarus got very sick. Mary and Martha sent a message to Jesus asking Him to come heal their brother. Even though Jesus loved His three friends, He waited two days to start the trip to see them, and Lazarus died before Jesus got there.

Martha and Mary said, "If You had come earlier, our brother wouldn't have died." Jesus was so sad He cried. Then He went to the tomb of Lazarus. He said, "Lazarus, come out!" And out came Lazarus, wrapped in the burial cloths. He was alive and well!

Sometimes when we ask Jesus for something, we have to wait—sometimes for a long time.

One Man Says Thank You

Luke 17:11–19

Ten men met Jesus as He was walking along a road. They didn't come close to Jesus because they had the horrible skin disease, leprosy. They called out, "Please help us!" Jesus told them they were healed and sent them on their way.

As the men went on their way, the leprosy disappeared. Only one man came back. He bowed down to Jesus and thanked Him for what He had done.

We should remember to say thank you for what God has done for us. What has God done for you?

Jesus Borrows a Donkey

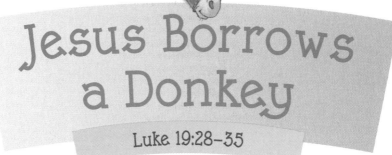

Luke 19:28–35

The first Passover happened when God's people left Egypt long ago. After that, God's people celebrated the Passover every year. One year Jesus and His closest followers went to Jerusalem to celebrate the Passover.

Before they got there, Jesus said to His followers, "Go into town and find a young donkey colt. Untie it and bring it to Me. If anyone asks where you are taking it, say, 'The Master needs it.'" When the men got back with the donkey colt, they spread their coats on its back. Jesus climbed on the colt.

Why do you suppose Jesus needed that donkey colt?

Jesus Rides Like a King

Luke 19:36–38; John 12:12–16

The donkey started to clippity-clop
through the town. People came running.
They threw their coats down for the
donkey to walk on. They took palm
branches and waved them in the air.
"Praise God!" they shouted.

362

Some of them remembered the Scriptures that said, "Your king is coming . . . sitting on the colt of a donkey."

Why do you suppose they laid their coats down
for the donkey to walk on?
Did they think Jesus was a king?

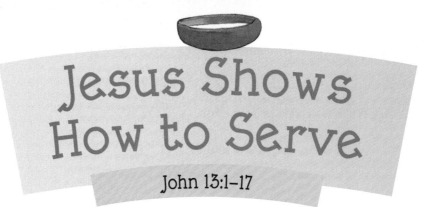

Jesus Shows How to Serve

John 13:1–17

Soon it was time for the Passover dinner. Jesus and His closest followers gathered in a big room. Jesus stood up, took off His coat, got some water in a wash bowl, and wrapped a towel around His waist.

Then He started washing His followers' feet. Jesus did this to teach His friends they were to serve one another.

Jesus was serving His followers to set a good example. What could you do to serve your brothers and sisters and parents?

The First Lord's Supper

Matthew 26:26–29; 1 Corinthians 11:23–25

While Jesus and His closest followers were eating the Passover dinner, Jesus took some bread and thanked God for it. He broke the bread apart and said, "Take this bread and eat it. Do this to remember Me."

Next He took a cup and said, "When you drink this juice of the grape, remember Me." Jesus knew this was His last meal with His followers because He was about to be killed. He wanted His followers to always remember Him.

Today in church we still eat bread and drink the juice of the grape to remember Jesus. We call this time of remembering *Communion* or *The Lord's Supper*.

Jesus Prays for Help

Matthew 26:36–40; Mark 14:32–42;
Luke 22:39–46

Jesus and His followers went straight
from dinner to a quiet garden. Jesus
wanted to pray and ask God to make
Him strong for what was about
to happen. He took three of
His closest followers—Peter,
James, and John—with him.
Jesus asked them to
wait and pray.

He went a little farther into the garden so that He could pray by Himself. It was very late, and the three men were very tired. They couldn't keep their eyes open to pray. Soon they were asleep. Jesus woke them twice, but they went back to sleep each time.

When we have tough things ahead of us, we need to pray and ask God to help us.

Jesus Is Arrested

Matthew 26:45–56; Luke 22:45–51; John 18:10–11

The third time Jesus woke His followers, He said, "We must go. Here comes the man who has turned against Me." Just then a big crowd carrying torches and clubs came into the garden. Judas, one of Jesus' followers, was with them. He kissed Jesus on the cheek. It was a signal to the guards to arrest Jesus.

Peter pulled out his sword and cut off the ear of one guard. Jesus told Peter to put the sword away. Then He healed the guard's ear.

You might think the crowd would let Jesus go after He healed the man's ear. Well, they didn't. They arrested Him and took Him away.

Pilate Questions Jesus

Luke 22:52–23:25

Lots of people loved Jesus, but there were many who didn't like Him at all. After Jesus was captured in the garden, He was taken to the house of the high priest, then to Pilate, the Roman governor of Judea.

All night the rulers asked Jesus if He was God's Son. They did not believe that He was. Finally Pilate said that he didn't think Jesus was guilty. But the people who hated Jesus kept yelling until Pilate decided that Jesus had to die on a cross.

Jesus told everyone that He was God's Son, and that made some people very angry. But even if they didn't believe it, He was still God's Son.

Jesus Is Killed on a Cross

Matthew 27:27–40; Mark 15:25–27

Pilate's soldiers took Jesus and put a crown of thorns on His head and made fun of Him. Then they led Jesus out of the city to a place called Golgotha to be killed on a cross.

374

At nine o'clock in the morning, the soldiers nailed Jesus to the cross. They also put two robbers beside Jesus, one on the right and one on the left.

The day God's Son died on the cross was a sad day.
But God had a wonderful plan.
Keep reading and you'll see what it was.

A Dark Day

Matthew 27:45–54; Luke 23:44–49;
Hebrews 9

While Jesus was on the cross, the land
became dark from noon until three
o'clock. Then Jesus died, and there was a
big earthquake.

376

When the earth shook, the thick curtain in the Temple between the Holy Place and the Most Holy Place ripped from top to bottom. Now people could see inside the Most Holy Place. Before, only the High Priest got to see inside. When the soldiers at the cross saw what happened when Jesus died, they knew He really was the Son of God!

Jesus died because He loved us. He died so that our sins could be forgiven. Let's tell Him right now that we love Him for what He did on the cross.

Jesus Is Laid in a Tomb

Luke 23:50–56

A rich man, named Joseph of Arimathea, had a new tomb where he had planned to be buried. He took Jesus' body from the cross and put it in his own empty tomb.

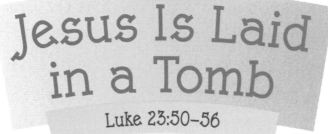

Joseph and Jesus' friends wrapped His body in strips of linen and laid it carefully in the tomb. Roman soldiers came to guard the tomb. They rolled a huge stone over the door and sealed it in a way that would show if anyone tried to move the stone.

Everyone thought that since Jesus was dead, they would never see Him again. They were in for a big surprise!

A Big Surprise

Matthew 28:1–10

The day after Jesus was buried was a holy day, so His friends had to stay home. Then very early on Sunday morning, the first day of the week, the women went back to the tomb. It was the third day since Jesus died.

When the women got there, they couldn't believe their eyes. The stone had been rolled away! An angel of God was sitting on the stone! The soldiers were so frightened they were like dead men.

How do you think those women at the tomb felt when they saw the angel?

Jesus Is Alive!

Matthew 28:5–8; Luke 24:9–12

The angel said, "Don't be afraid. Jesus is alive." Those women were as happy as they could be! They ran to find other friends of Jesus.

Some of Jesus' friends didn't believe what the women said. But everything the women said was true. Jesus was alive! He had risen from death.

How long is forever? Jesus promised He would come back to life . . . and He did. Jesus is alive today and will be forever.

Jesus Eats Dinner with Two Friends

Luke 24:13–32

Two of Jesus' friends were walking along the road, and Jesus joined them. These two people didn't know it was Jesus who was walking with them. But they liked talking with this man.

They invited Him to have dinner at their house. Jesus came, and while He was thanking God for the food, the friends realized the man was Jesus. Then Jesus disappeared.

After Jesus was raised from the dead, He could appear and disappear. What would you do if Jesus suddenly appeared here?

Jesus Appears to a Room Full of Friends

Luke 24:33–49

One night Jesus appeared in a room where many of His friends were gathered. He told them to tell their family and friends and neighbors and even strangers that He is alive.

He told them to share everything He had taught them. They were to tell the people in Jerusalem first, but then they were to tell people everywhere. Jesus told them to wait in Jerusalem until God sent them a special gift of power from heaven.

Whom do you know that would like to hear all about Jesus' love?

Jesus Goes to Heaven

Luke 24:50–53; Acts 1:6–11

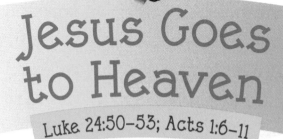

Jesus led His followers a little way out of town. Jesus prayed for His followers, and while He was praying, He started to rise up into heaven. Then a cloud hid Him from His followers.

388

As everyone was standing there staring up into heaven, two angels appeared beside them and said, "Jesus has been taken away from you and into heaven. He will come back in the clouds, just like He went away."

Remember the gift that God was going to send?
Keep reading and see what happened.

God's Spirit Comes to Help

Acts 2:1–4

After Jesus went back to heaven,
His friends and helpers were praying
together in a big room. Suddenly
something amazing happened.

First it sounded as if a huge wind were blowing. Next flames of fire flickered over every person's head. Then God's Spirit came, and everyone began to speak in different languages. This was the gift from God that Jesus had promised His followers.

Jesus' friends were happy. God's Spirit had come to live with them and to help them.

Everyone Hears and Understands

Acts 2:5–42

The night that God's Spirit came to Jesus' followers, there were people from many countries in Jerusalem. These people spoke different languages.

When they heard Jesus' friends praying, they went to see what the noise was all about. They found Jesus' friends telling about the great things God had done.

But they were all surprised to hear it in their own language. "What does this mean?" they asked.

God's Holy Spirit still helps those who follow Jesus today.

A Beggar at the Temple

Acts 2:43–3:10

After that day when the Holy Spirit first
came, Jesus' followers began to do many
miracles, telling people about God's love
and how Jesus had come to save them.
One afternoon Peter and John went to the
Temple. A man who couldn't walk sat there
begging for money. Peter looked at him
and said, "I don't have any money, but I do
have something else I can give you: By the
power of Jesus Christ from Nazareth—
stand up and walk!" Up jumped the man.
His feet and ankles were now strong.

Do you know someone who is sick? Now is a good time to pray and ask Jesus to help them.

Philip Meets an Ethiopian

Acts 8:26–31

Philip was another one of Jesus'
followers. He was busy telling people
about Jesus when an angel spoke to
him. "Go out on the road,"
the angel said. Along came
a very important man
from Ethiopia riding in
his chariot. He was
reading from the
book of Isaiah.

Philip ran alongside the chariot and said, "Do you understand what you are reading?" No, the man didn't understand. He stopped the chariot and invited Philip to ride in the chariot and explain what the book meant.

God looks for people, like Philip, who are ready to do what He asks.

Philip Baptizes the Ethiopian

Acts 8:32–40

Philip explained the Scripture passage the man was reading. It was all about Jesus. The man asked, "Why don't I get baptized?" The Ethiopian man believed in Jesus, and he wanted to be baptized.

So they stopped the chariot, and Philip baptized him. Then God needed Philip in another place, and *whoosh!* Just like that, Philip was gone.

When we do what God asks of us, we don't know what will happen next. We just need to be ready for whatever it is.

A Mean Man

Acts 9:1–4

There was a mean man chasing after Jesus' followers. His name was Saul. He was sure that everything he heard about Jesus was wrong. He didn't believe any of it. He was sure he was right. So he hurt, and even killed, people who believed in Jesus.

Well, God wanted Saul to work for Him. So one day when Saul was on a journey, God sent a bright flash of light. It was so bright, Saul fell to the ground.

Why do you think God wanted Saul to work for Him?

Saul Is Blinded

Acts 9:4–9

"Saul! Why are you doing things against Me?" a voice said from inside the light. "Who are you?" asked Saul. "I am Jesus. Now get up and go into the city."

When Saul stood up, he was blind. His friends had to lead him into the city. Saul wouldn't eat or drink anything for three days.

What will happen to poor, blind Saul?
Do you think he is ready to listen to God?

Ananias Helps Saul

Acts 9:10–18; 13:9

God sent a man named Ananias to find
Saul and pray for him so that Saul could
see again. Ananias was scared of Saul.
But Ananias believed in Jesus and went
anyway.

Ananias prayed for Saul, and Saul's sight came back. On that day, God changed Saul's heart to make him kind to those who believed in Jesus. Saul was also called Paul. Soon Paul began to tell others about Jesus too.

Did you know that Paul became one of the greatest preachers who ever lived?

Peter in Jail

Acts 12:1–18

One day mean King Herod threw Peter,
one of Jesus' followers, in jail. The
king had 16 soldiers guard Peter so
he couldn't get away. That night an
angel came into Peter's cell. "Hurry!
Get up!" the angel said. "Follow me."
Peter thought he must be dreaming
. . . but he wasn't. The chains fell
off his hands, and the angel led him
past the guards. When they came to
the iron gate of the prison, it swung
open on its own, and Peter was free.

God is always stronger than anything that can happen to us. We have to trust that He will always do what's best for us.

A Woman Who Sold Purple Cloth

Acts 16:12–15

After Paul became a follower of Jesus, he went everywhere teaching people about Jesus. Many times there was no building where he could meet with friends. One day he and his friends were looking for a place to meet by the river when they saw a group of women.

One woman was Lydia. Her job was selling purple cloth. She loved God, but didn't know about Jesus. Paul told her all about Jesus, and Lydia believed that Jesus was God's Son. Lydia invited Paul and his friends to stay at her house.

Some of your friends probably want to know Jesus. They are just waiting for someone to tell them about Him. You could be the one who tells them.

Earthquake!

Acts 16:16–36

Some people didn't like what Paul was preaching about Jesus. So they caught Paul and his helper, Silas, and threw them in jail. The two men were beaten, and their feet were fastened tightly so they couldn't run away. That night, instead of complaining or crying, Paul and Silas prayed and sang songs to God.

Suddenly there was an earthquake, and the jail doors popped open. The jailer thought his prisoners had escaped. He knew if the prisoners had escaped, he would be in big trouble. Paul called to him, "We are all here!" When the jailer came to them, he asked, "What must I do to be saved?" Paul told him all about Jesus.

If you had been beaten, thrown in jail, and had your feet pinned down, what would you be doing?

Some People Laugh at Paul

Acts 17:16–34

Paul traveled to Athens in Greece to tell people about Jesus. In Athens, Paul saw an altar with writing that said, "TO A GOD WHO IS NOT KNOWN." Paul began to preach. He told the people about the God who made the whole world.

Paul said that God doesn't live in temples that men build, but in their hearts. He told them about Jesus coming back to life after being dead. Some of the people laughed at Paul, but some of the people believed in Jesus.

TO A GOD WHO IS NOT KNOWN.

God wants all of us to tell others the Good News that Jesus is alive. Some people will believe, and some will laugh. We must pray for all of them.

Shipwrecked!

Paul got on a big ship. He was going to the city of Rome. The ship went very slowly because of strong winds blowing against it. Finally, the ship came to a safe harbor, and Paul told the captain he didn't think it was a good idea to leave the harbor for a while. But the captain disagreed, and he sailed anyway.

Soon a wind came up and blew hard on the ship. The sailors couldn't steer it. Paul knew they were in trouble—they might sink. He told the sailors to eat so they would be strong for the trouble ahead. Before long, the ship hit a sandbank and began to break into pieces. Everyone had to jump into the sea and swim for the beach. They all made it to shore safely.

How scary! A shipwreck! Where did they land? What happened next?

A Poisonous Snake

Acts 28:1–6

All the people from the shipwreck were now on the island of Malta, near the country of Greece. The people who lived on the island were very kind. They built a fire and invited the passengers to warm themselves.

Paul helped by gathering wood for the fire, and as he did, a poisonous snake bit him on the hand. Paul just shook the snake off into the fire. He was not even hurt. The island people waited for him to fall down dead from the poison, but Paul was just fine.

Why do you think Paul did not die when the poisonous snake bit him?

New Heaven and Earth

Revelation 21

One of the biggest promises God ever
made was that we will live with Him
in heaven forever. He said that there
would be a new heaven and a new earth
and we would get a new body—one that
won't get old but will live forever.

418

In the new heaven, no one will ever be sad again. No one will ever die again. The streets will be made of gold, and there will be gates of pearl. Everything will be more beautiful than anything you can imagine. And best of all, Jesus will be there. We will be with Him forever.

What is the most beautiful thing you have ever seen? Heaven will be a thousand times more beautiful.

A Promise to All God's Children

"No one has ever seen this.
No one has ever heard about it.
No one has ever imagined
what God has prepared
for those who love him."

1 Corinthians 2:9